4

We give people presents on their birthday. Pete's mum and dad gave him a bicycle. His brother, Ant, helped them to choose it.

" Ant says...

"I went with Mum to the shop. I knew Pete would like a yellow bike."

Joe gave his brother a fun game on his birthday.

Annie and Patrick gave
their granny bubble bath.

Your turn...

Why do you think families
give each other presents?

It's nice to give birthday cards, too. Mingyu made a card for her mum.

Lotte drew a boat for her dad.

Lotte says...
"Dad always says he wants a boat."

Birthdays are days for
special treats. Lee's mum
took him and his friends
to the zoo.

Lois spent her birthday
in the park.

? Your turn...

What special treat would you
like on your birthday?

Annie and Karl took their mum breakfast in bed on her birthday.

" Karl says...
"Mum ate it all up -
even the burnt bits!"

13

Lots of people have birthday parties. Hayley's aunt came before her party to help with the cooking.

? Your turn...

Have you had a birthday party?
Who helped to get it ready?
What food did you have?

Jagdish had fun at his birthday party. His friends and family came. There was a clown.

> **Jagdish says...**
> "We all laughed a lot."

17

On Nia's first birthday, all the family helped blow out the candle on her cake.

Paul blew out all the candles on his own.

? Your turn...

What do people sing when they light the candles on a birthday cake?

Some birthdays are more important than others. All the family got together for Aidan's grandad's 70th birthday.

Aidan says...

"Everyone was there – my mum, dad, sister and gran and all my uncles, aunts and cousins. Grandad looked really pleased."

How do you and your family celebrate your birthday?

Some things to do

When is your birthday? When are your family and friends' birthdays? Collect together the dates and make a birthday book.

Pretend it is someone in your family's birthday and plan a surprise party for them. Make lists of who you will invite, what food you will eat and what games you will play.

Design a birthday card for someone in your family, with a picture of something he or she likes.

Write a poem or tell a story about the best birthday present ever.

About this book

The aim of this book is to give children the opportunity to explore what their family means to them and their role within it in a positive and celebratory way. In particular it emphasises the importance of care and support within the family. It also encourages children to compare their own experiences with other people, recognising similarities and differences and respecting these as part of daily life.

Children will get pleasure out of looking at this book on their own. However, sharing the book on a one-to-one basis or within a group will also be very rewarding. Just talking about the main text and pictures is a good starting point, while the panels also prompt discussion:
• Question panels ask children to talk directly about their own experiences and feelings.
• Quote panels encourage them to think further by comparing their experiences with those of other children.

This edition 2010

Franklin Watts, 338 Euston Road
London NW1 3BH

Franklin Watts Australia
Level 17/207 Kent Street, Sydney NSW 2000

Copyright © Franklin Watts 2007

Dewey classification: 394.2
ISBN: 978 0 7496 9608 5

Series editor: Rachel Cooke
Art director: Jonathan Hair
Design: Jason Anscomb

Picture credits: Meiko Arquillos/zefa/Corbis: 9. John-Francis Bourke/zefa/Corbis: 14. Gareth Brown/Corbis: 8. Owen Franken/Corbis: 18. Grace/zefa/Corbis: 3 Sally Greenhill/Sally & Richard Greenhill: 10, 21. Richard Hutchings/Corbis: Cover, 22. Richard T. Nowitz/Corbis: 6. Ulrike Preuss/Photofusion: 11, 17. Paula Solloway /Photofusion: 19. LWA-Dann Tardif/Corbis: 13. Bob Watkins/Photofusion: 7. Stephanie Weiler/zefa/Corbis: 4. Every attempt has been made to clear copyright. Should there be any inadvertent omission please apply to the publisher for rectification.

Please note that some of the pictures in this book have been posed by models.

Printed in China

Franklin Watts is a division of Hachette Children's Books, an Hachette UK company.
www.hachette.co.uk